# Heritage Studies 1

### for Christian Schools®
### SECOND EDITION

## The New World

At Home in Early America

# Kimberly H. Pascoe and Dawn L. Watkins

Bob Jones University Press, Greenville, South Carolina 29614

NOTE:
The fact that materials produced by other publishers are referred to in this volume does not constitute an endorsement by Bob Jones University Press of the content or theological position of materials produced by such publishers. The position of the Bob Jones University Press, and the University itself, is well known. Any references and ancillary materials are listed as an aid to the student or teacher and in an attempt to maintain the accepted academic standards of the publishing industry.

**HERITAGE STUDIES 1 for Christian Schools® Second Edition**
**The New World: At Home in Early America**

Kimberly H. Pascoe
Dawn L. Watkins

Produced in cooperation with the Bob Jones University Department of Social Studies Education, the College of Arts and Science, and Bob Jones Elementary School

© 1996 Bob Jones University Press
Greenville, South Carolina 29614
First Edition © 1979

ISBN  0-89084-880-7

15  14  13  12  11  10 9 8 7 6 5 4 3 2 1

# Contents

Geography

American History

Government

Economics

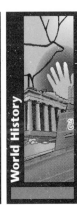
World History

Culture

# 1

# Water and Land

*And God called
the dry land Earth;
and the gathering
together of the waters
called he Seas: and
God saw that it was
good.*

Genesis 1:10

When do you see puddles?
A puddle is some water in a
low place.
Why are some puddles bigger
than others?

Here is a puddle
in the parking lot.

Have you ever seen a pond?
A pond is like a huge puddle.
It is a lot of water in a low place.

What do you think a lake is?

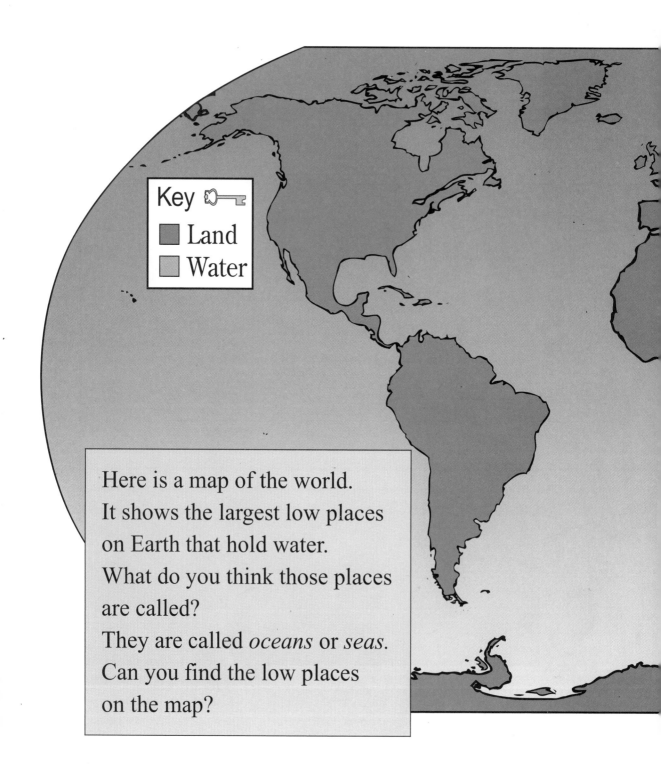

Key

Land
Water

Here is a map of the world.
It shows the largest low places
on Earth that hold water.
What do you think those places
are called?
They are called *oceans* or *seas*.
Can you find the low places
on the map?

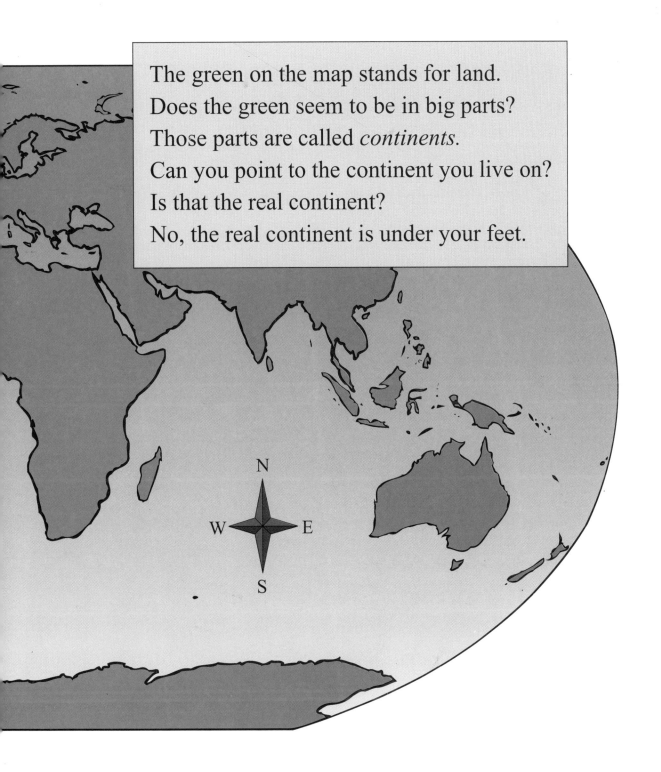

The green on the map stands for land.

Does the green seem to be in big parts?

Those parts are called *continents*.

Can you point to the continent you live on?

Is that the real continent?

No, the real continent is under your feet.

Sailors from the continent of Europe did not
have maps like yours.
Their maps looked more like the one
on this page.
How is it different from your maps?
Do you see the cross on this page?
It shows north, east, south, and west.
These are directions.

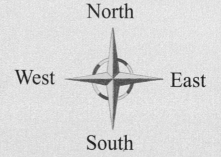

## To Find Directions

1. Go outside just before sunset. Look for the sun.

2. Hold your left arm straight out from your side. Hold your left palm up toward the sun, as though you were an officer stopping traffic. Now you are facing north.

3. What direction is behind you?
   What direction is on your right?

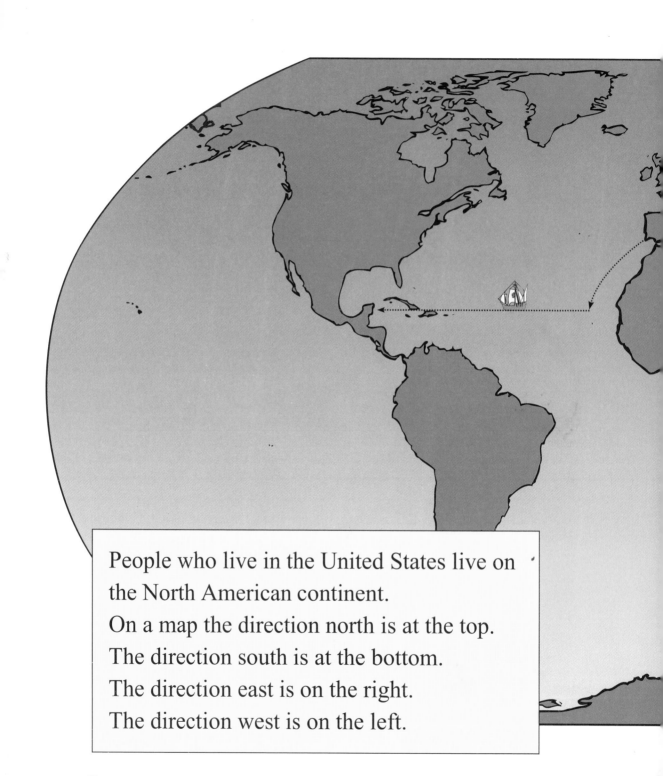

People who live in the United States live on
the North American continent.
On a map the direction north is at the top.
The direction south is at the bottom.
The direction east is on the right.
The direction west is on the left.

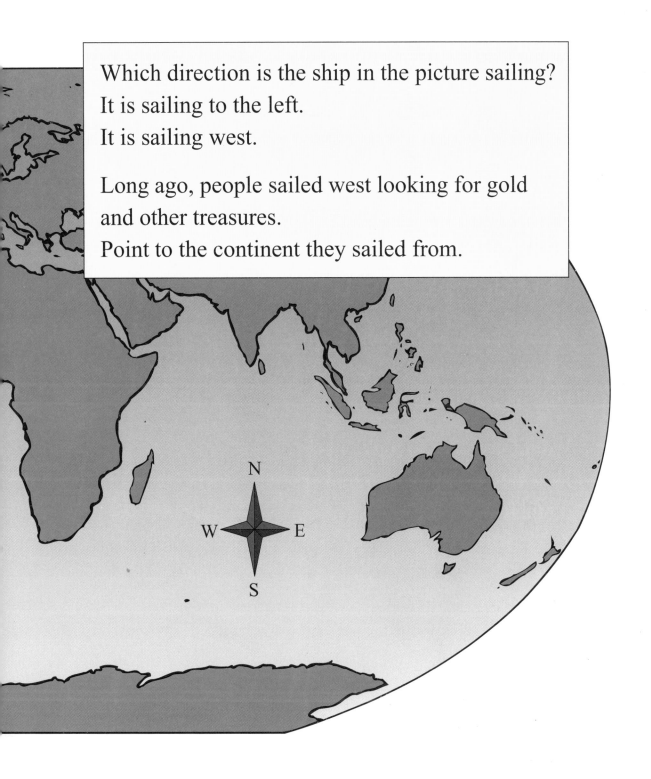

Which direction is the ship in the picture sailing?
It is sailing to the left.
It is sailing west.

Long ago, people sailed west looking for gold
and other treasures.
Point to the continent they sailed from.

## Making Maps

Long ago, people made drawings of places as
they traveled.
The next people to travel in the same places tried
to make the map drawings better.
Sometimes people had to guess how the edges of
the continents looked.

Today spaceships take pictures of Earth.
The pictures show us exactly how the water and
land on Earth look.

Would you like to make maps?
How do you think mapmakers
do their work today?

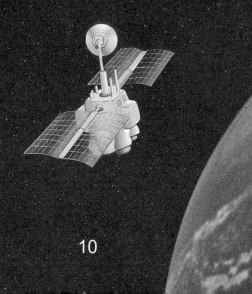

People use the oceans to travel from
place to place.
How else can people get from place to place?
Why do you think people want to go from one
place to another?
Sometimes people want a warmer place to live.
Sometimes they want to do different
kinds of work.

People use the directions north, east, south, and west to find their way from place to place. Look at the map on this page.

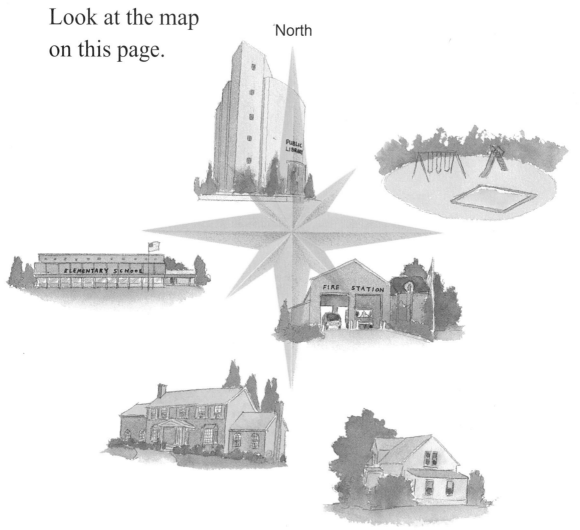

Which way would you tell someone to go who wanted to go from the school to the playground? Should the person go east, west, north, or south?

## Leif Ericson

Leif Ericson's father
was a Viking sailor.
Leif sailed on his
father's ship.
He learned to find
his direction by the
stars and sun.
When Leif grew up,
he sailed his own ship.
He explored North
America hundreds of
years ago.

## To Read a Map

1. Take out your Notebook, some colored pencils, and a ruler.

2. Take out the Notebook page your teacher tells you to.

3. Answer the questions your teacher asks by looking at the map. Use the pencils to color the map as your teacher tells you.

# 2
# Columbus and His Ships

Many, many years ago men did not have maps
like we have today.
Their maps showed only the land they had seen.
How many continents can you find on this map?
It shows Europe, Africa, and Asia.

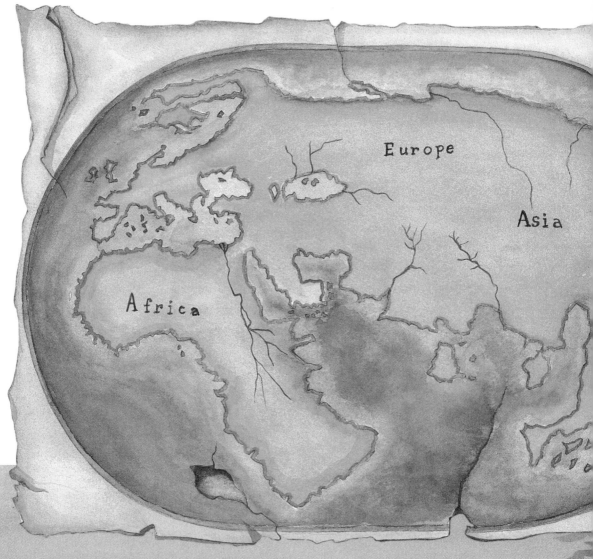

*It is he that sitteth upon the circle of the earth.* Isaiah 40:22

What special kind of map do we use to show the whole world? We use a globe. Many years ago, people did not use globes.

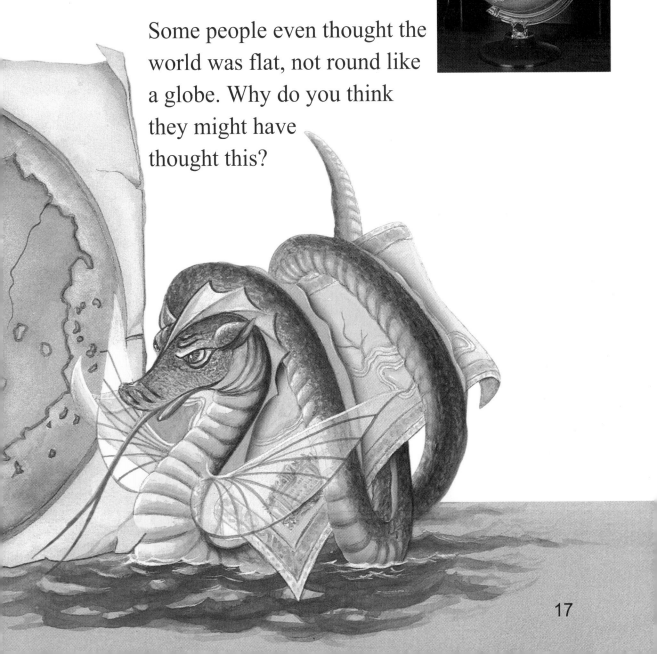

Some people even thought the world was flat, not round like a globe. Why do you think they might have thought this?

# Christopher Columbus

Christopher Columbus lived in a big city.
He liked to watch the ships sail in and out
of the harbor.
He wanted to be the captain of a big ship.
When he grew up, Christopher made maps.
He sailed many places. He read many books.
The writers of the books said the world
was round.
"I believe the world is round too,"
thought Christopher.

# To Make a Map

1. Gather some colored pencils, a ruler, and a large piece of paper.

2. Make a map showing where things are in your classroom. Use symbols to show where desks, bookcases, and other things are.

3. How is your map like the maps Columbus made? How is it different?

In those days men were trying to find a way to
reach Asia by ship.

They tried to sail down the coast of Africa
and around it.

But Christopher said, "There is another way
to Asia. I want to sail across the great ocean."

He thought he knew a shorter way to bring back
beautiful things from that faraway land.

# Before the King and Queen

Christopher Columbus needed money
to make his trip.
What might he need money for?

Columbus went to see the king of the country
where he lived.
He asked the king to give him money for ships.
He told the king, "I will find a shorter way to
Asia for you."

The king laughed.
"The distance to Asia is greater than you think.
And you ask for too much money. I will not
help you."

Do you think Columbus gave up?
No. Columbus thought, "I will not let him
stop me."
He went to see the king and queen
of another country.
He asked them to help.

King Ferdinand and Queen Isabella thought
about what Columbus said.
They talked with their helpers.
The king and queen took eight years to decide.
Finally they told Columbus, "Yes, we will
help you."

What do you think Columbus did next?
He found three ships that could make a long trip.
He found eighty-nine men who were not afraid
to sail with him.

## Building Ships

Long ago, men made ships from wood.
They cut and shaped the wood.
They nailed the pieces together to make the ship.
Then they rolled the ship to the water on a cart.

Today, most ships are not made of wood. They are made from steel. Many hundreds of people work to build each ship.

# The New World

The sailors were afraid.
The ships had been sailing for more than
one month.
Many men grumbled and complained.
"We should have reached Asia by now,"
they said.
"Maybe the world *is* flat."
They wanted to turn back.

Columbus did not listen to the men.
He said, "I will punish anyone who grumbles."
Then he told them the king and queen had
promised to reward the first man to see land.

The next day someone did see land.
It happened very early in the morning.
The sun was not up yet.
The other men were still sleeping.
"Land!" he yelled. "Land!"

Christopher Columbus had seen land. He thought he had come to a part of Asia called *India*. He called the people he met *Indians*. But those people did not call themselves Indians.

Columbus made three more ocean trips. Each time he looked for the spices and soft cloth. He never understood that he had not found a new way to India. Now we remember Columbus on *Columbus Day*.

One hundred years later, Spanish people built towns far from where Columbus had been. They were on the other side of the New World. The Spanish called their place New Mexico. Some of that land is still called New Mexico.

# Amerigo Vespucci

Amerigo Vespucci sailed across the ocean as
Columbus did.

He wrote a book about the new lands
he had seen.

He did not think that these lands were part
of Asia.

He said they were a "new world."

This New World was named after Amerigo.

We call it
*America*.

AMERICAE SIVE
NOVI ORBIS, NO
VA DESCRIPTIO.

28

# 3

# People of
# the New World

Columbus called the people he met
in the New World *Indians*.
Why did he give them this name?
Before Columbus came, the people he
met called themselves by another name.
They called themselves *Arawaks*.
Only the Arawaks and one other group of
people lived on the tiny islands Columbus saw.

But many, many groups of people lived
on the continents in the New World.
Some lived in the forests.
Some lived on the flat, grassy plains.
Some lived near the ocean.
And some lived in the dry and
sandy deserts.

Do you think these
people had other names
for themselves too?

# Woodland Peoples

Woodland people lived in the forest.
Most Woodland people were farmers.
They cut down some of the trees.
Then they planted vegetables.

Woodland people made canoes from trees.
Woodland people hunted for animals
in the forest.
What do you think the people did with the
animals they killed?
They ate the meat and used the skins to make
clothes and shoes.

*Every moving thing that liveth shall be meat for you;
even as the green herb have I given you all things.*

Genesis 9:3

# Making Tools

The people made everything
they needed before
Columbus came.
They made *tools* from
wood and stone or
animal bone.
Tools are things people use
to help them do work.
What tools do you use?

They made axes and knives
from stone and bits of bone.
They used the axes to cut down
trees and to make canoes.
They used stone or bone
to make needles for sewing.
They made arrows
from stone or bone too.
What did they use the arrows for?

The *Calusa* were one group of Woodland people.
They lived in swampy forests.
The weather was always warm where the
Calusa lived.
Do you think they needed
heavy clothes?

The Calusa built homes from woven grass mats.
The Calusa cut tall, dry grass to make the roofs.
Grass roofs kept their homes dry.

The *Iroquois* were another group of
Woodland people.
The Iroquois were really five small groups made
into one very large group.

They called themselves
"People of the Long House."
Why do you think they called
themselves by that name?
The Iroquois built very long houses from
wooden poles and bark.
Many families lived in each house.

# Plains Peoples

The Plains people lived on the flat, grassy plains.
Few trees grew on the plains.
Few animals lived on the plains.
How do you think these people got their food
and clothing?
What kind of homes could they build?

The *Sioux* were one group of Plains people.
They hunted buffalo.
Hunting buffalo gave them the things
they needed.
They ate the buffalo meat.
They made tools from the buffalo's bones.
They used the buffalo's skin to make clothes
and shoes.
They even made their homes from these skins.
Do you know what this kind of home is called?
It is called a *tipi*.

# Playing Games

The people in the New World played
many games.

They played games with balls.

They played games with sticks and
games with strings.

They played guessing games.

They played many games that we play today.

Men played some games.

Women played some games.

Some games were played by both men
and women.

Children had their own games.

Some played a special game with a ball.

They called it "little brother of war."

Only the very brave men played that game.

# Arctic Peoples

The *Inuit* lived in the north lands. They fished in the cold water. They hunted for bears and seals and whales.

During the winter, the Inuit lived in homes of ice and snow.
During the summer, they built homes from mud and sticks.
They called their homes *igloos*.
The Inuit were once called *Eskimos*.

# Northwest Coast Peoples

The *Nootka* were one group of Northwest Coast
people.
The Nootka lived near the ocean.
They lived near the forest too.
They used the tall, strong trees to make
giant canoes.
They used the canoes when fishing and hunting
whales on the ocean.

The Nootka also used the tall, strong trees to make warm homes.

The Nootka homes were long.

What other Indian group built long homes?

The Nootka made a special object for their long homes.

Tall posts stood at each corner.

They cut the posts to look like different animals.

Each home had different animals cut in its posts.

The giant post in the center of one side had a hole in it.

What do you think the hole was for?

## Southwest Peoples

The Southwest people lived in the hot, dry desert.
They were farmers.
They ate the vegetables that they grew.
They made beautiful things from the plants.

The *Hopi* built homes from dried mud.
They built their homes on top of one another.
What do their homes look like to you?

# To Make an Indian Weaving

1. Gather two or more colors of construction paper, a pair of scissors, a ruler, a pencil, and some glue or tape.

2. Use the ruler to draw straight, thick lines on the pieces of construction paper.

3. Fold one piece of paper in half. Cut along the straight lines from the folded edge. Stop cutting each line before you reach the edge of the paper. Unfold the paper.

4. Cut the other pieces of paper into long strips along the straight lines. Weave these strips over and under the strips on the unfolded piece of paper. Decorate the weaving with Indian designs.

Today, some groups live
just as people lived
long ago.
But most do not.
They do not make things
from wood and stone.
They do not build homes
from bark or buffalo skin.

But we remember things the early people did.
We remember things they taught the people who
came to the New World.
And we remember that they were
the first Americans.

# 4

## New Homes in the New World

What is a *settlement?*

A settlement is a group of people living in a new place. The group of people make up a town or a city.

Do you remember who built the first settlements in the New World? Native Americans did.

**NORTH AMERICA**

Many years after Columbus came to the New World, white men began to build settlements there. Many of these people went to live in the northern part of the New World. Today, we call the northern part of the New World *North America.*

## The Lost Settlement

Ships brought men and women and children
to the New World.
They built the first English settlement.
Then they sent the ships back to get more food
and people.
When the ships came back, the people
were gone.
What do you think happened to the people?
Most people think they went to live
with the Indians.

## Sir Walter Raleigh

Sir Walter Raleigh was a soldier and a seaman.
He wanted to take settlers to the New World.
Queen Elizabeth of England would not let
Sir Walter go.
But she did let him send the first settlers.
And she helped him pay for the ships and food.

The settlement that Sir Walter paid for was lost.
No one knows what happened to the settlers.

## Jamestown

Three small ships sailed up a river
on a warm day in May 1607.
Why do you think those ships were there?
The ships carried one hundred five men
from England.
These men had come to live in North America.
They came to hunt for gold.
They wanted to become rich.

The men named the river the James River, after their king.
They called the place they landed *Jamestown.*
Why do you think they gave it that name?
Do you think it had another name first?
Most of the men in Jamestown came from rich families.
They did not know how to work hard.
They thought they would find gold in the new land.
They hoped it would be easy to find.
They would go back to England when they had found lots of gold.
Do you think they found gold?

Captain John Smith was one of the leaders
in Jamestown.
He worked with the men to build houses
and a church.
How were these houses different from the house
you live in?
The men covered twigs and planks with mud
to make the walls.
They made the roofs of straw or grass.

Captain Smith also worked with the men to plant crops.

He told them that if they did not work, they could not eat.

Was Captain Smith a wise leader?

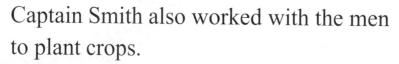

Some of the men worked very hard. But they were not used to life in the new land. The crops did not grow well. The men did not have enough food.

Many men became sick and died. By fall only thirty-eight men were left.

*If any would not work, neither should he eat.*

II Thessalonians 3:10

What do you think Captain Smith did then?
He went to the Indians for help.
He got corn and other food from the Indians.
Soon more men came from England.
They brought more food.
With help from the Indians and from England,
the men lived through the winter.

Still more men came from England in the spring.

Soon many men lived in Jamestown.

Even two ladies came with one group from England.

The men were not getting rich.

But the settlement grew.

# Growing Crops

The people in Jamestown had to grow food to eat. The Indians helped. They gave the men seeds to plant. The men learned to plant crops that would give food. They learned to plant crops that could be sold for money.

Today, people still need to grow food to eat. They still grow crops that can be sold for money. What do we call the people who grow crops? We call them *farmers*.

55

Each year more and more people came
to Jamestown.

Most of these people were white men.

But one ship brought ninety young ladies to live
in the settlement.

And another ship brought twenty black men.

What do you think happened to these men?

They were sold to white men in Jamestown.

They had to work hard for those men.

# To Plant a Crop

1. Gather some plastic cups or egg cartons, some soil, water, and some seeds.

2. Fill each cup or egg carton section with soil. Plant one seed in each cup or section.Pour a little water over the soil.

3. Observe your crops every day. Add a little water every few days.

4. How long does it take for the crops to grow? How long do you think it will be before the crops are ready to eat? Would you like to care for a whole field of your crop? What would you have to do differently?

Jamestown was the first lasting English
settlement in the New World.
Men soon built more settlements nearby.
The place where all these settlements were
found was called *Virginia*.
Have you heard that name before?
Today, Virginia is one of
the states in the
United States.

The State
of Virginia

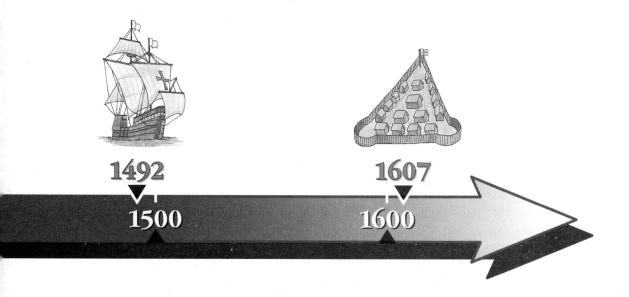

1492

1500

1607

1600

# 5

# God's Laws
# and Man's Laws

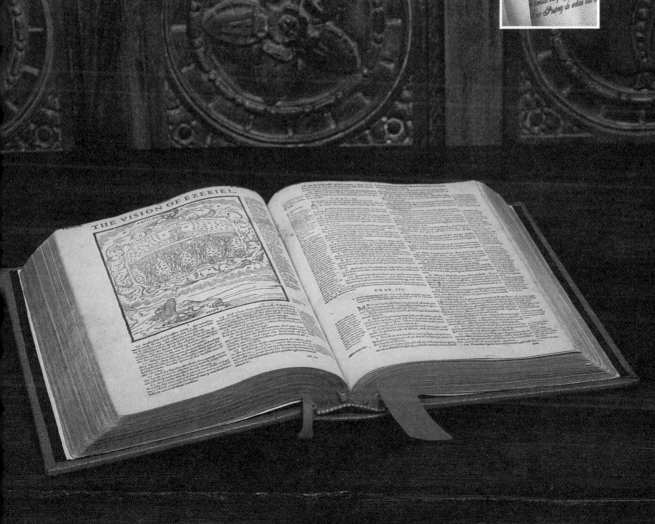

Would you like the president of the United States
to tell you which church to go to?
The king of England told his people that
everyone had to belong to the king's church.

Some English people did not go to
the king's church.
These people said, "We must obey God
in our worship."
They "separated" from the king's church.
They called themselves *Separatists*.

*Wherefore come
out from among
them, and be ye
separate.*

II Corinthians 6:17

The Separatists wanted to read
the Bible for themselves.
They wanted to worship
God as the Bible taught.
They wanted to have
their own church.

What do you
think they did?

The Separatists
hired a ship called
the *Mayflower*.

They sailed to the New World.

The *Mayflower* was small.
It was about as long as
eight average cars lined up.
It was about as wide as
four cars side by side.

There were 102 passengers
on the *Mayflower*.
Many were children.
Joseph Mullins was six years old.
So was the girl Remember Allerton.
A baby was born on the ship.
The captain had more than twenty men
in his crew.
How do you think all these people got along on
the small boat?

The crew made fun of the Separatists for
praying and singing hymns.
Do you think the people stopped praying
and singing?
No, they did not.

The Separatists landed in the New World.
The settlers called the place *Plymouth Plantation.*

The captain of the *Mayflower* kept saying,
"Hurry up! Find a place to stay."
He wanted to sail back to England.
At last the Separatists found a good place
to build houses.

Before the Separatists got off their ship,
they made some laws.
Why do you think people need laws?
Laws help people live together without trouble.
What laws do you know of in your town?

The Separatists signed their names to the laws.
They called their laws the *Mayflower Compact.*
A *compact* is an agreement, a promise.

# Anne Bradstreet

Only men wrote the Mayflower Compact.
But women in Plymouth also wrote.
They wrote letters back to England.
They wrote in diaries about things that happened
in everyday life.

Anne Bradstreet came over on a later ship
to a different town.
She was the first poet in America to have
a book published.
Some poems were about her children.

Many of her poems
were about her
home in the New
World.

Later, the Separatists chose William Bradford
to be governor, or leader.
He was wise and kind and fair.
Every year the Separatists elected him again.
He was governor thirty times.

William Bradford kept a book about Plymouth.
He wrote down everything that happened there.
His book tells us most of what we know
about those early settlers.

The first year in Plymouth Plantation was hard.
There was little food.
The Separatists hunted and fished some.
But it was too late in the year to plant
any vegetables.

The winter was cold and hard.
The snow fell, and the wind blew.
The people began to run out of food.
What do you think happened to the settlers?

A man named Squanto came to help.
He brought fish and corn.
He brought deer meat.

Squanto showed the settlers how to cook
the food.
He made a special Indian dish
of beans and corn.
Do you think the settlers
were grateful for his help?

In the spring the Indians taught the settlers how to plant corn.
They taught them how to get cod and clams.
Without Squanto and other Indians, the settlers might have died.

The next fall the Separatists stored much food for the coming winter.
They were grateful to God for their new home.
They were thankful for the people who had helped them.

The Separatists gave a great feast to show their thankfulness.

They invited all the Indians who had helped them.

Today we call this feast *Thanksgiving*.

*Giving thanks always for all things unto God and the Father in the name of our Lord Jesus Christ.*

Ephesians 5:20

# Celebrating Thanksgiving

Many people in the United States eat turkey
on Thanksgiving.
Why do you think they do that?
Turkey was part of the first Thanksgiving meal.

The Indians brought deer meat and fish
to the feast.
There was probably pumpkin pudding.
Do you have any food made of pumpkin
on Thanksgiving?

# To Make Indian Pudding

1. Take out the ingredients your teacher tells you to get. You will also need a baking dish, a saucepan, a wire whisk, and a place to bake the pudding.

2. Help your teacher mix the ingredients. How do you think the pudding will taste?

3. Bake the pudding. Taste the pudding. Do you think that you would have liked the food at the first Thanksgiving?

# 6
# Maps of Old Places

Cities usually start out as small towns.
Some start out as just a few houses.
A few have begun with one family
settling somewhere.

Do you know how your town or city started?
How could you find out?
One way is to ask someone who has lived in
your town a long time whether he knows how
the town grew.

Not all towns look alike.
Most towns add buildings as they are needed.
Is there a new building being put up
in your town?

The way a town looks tells us what the people
who live there think is important.
The town can also tell us something about how
the people live.

# Indian Towns

Indians had many kinds of villages and towns.
The Hopi people lived in houses made of
clay blocks.
The houses belonged to the women
of the village.

Some people made their houses in cliffs.
How do you think they got to their houses?

Other Indians made houses
from buffalo hides and poles.
The Sioux made such houses.
The houses were called *tipis*.

The Sioux drew pictures
of animals on the sides of their tipis.
Often they drew signs of bravery on a house.
Who do you think lived in such a tipi?

Squanto lived in a village near Plymouth Plantation. This is a map of his village. The houses are called *wigwams.*
How many wigwams do you see?

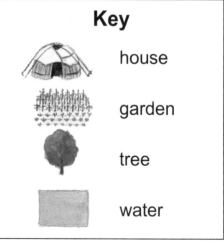

**Key**

house

garden

tree

water

What is growing near each wigwam?
Why do you think the Indians built their village here?

# Squanto

Squanto spoke English when he first met
the Separatists.

How did he know English?
He had been taken to England
by a sea captain years before.
He came back to his own home
on Captain John Smith's ship.
Then Squanto was taken
by another white man to Spain.
He got away and went
to England.
Still another sea captain brought
him back to his home
in the New World.
But Squanto did not
hate white men.
He believed what the
Separatists told him
about God.

# Finding Old Towns

Letters and books of long ago tell of towns that
do not stand anymore.
People try to find the old towns with maps
from the books.
They have to dig into the ground to find where
houses once were.
Sometimes they build a model of the town
they find.

# Jamestown

When it was first built, Jamestown may have looked like this.

How many houses do you see?

Why do you think there is a
wall around the town?
Look at the building in the center of the town.
What do you see on the front of the roof?
What do you think the building was?

This is a map of Jamestown.

Is Jamestown near the water?

Can you find the church on the map?

What do you see in each corner of the town?

Look at the key to find out.

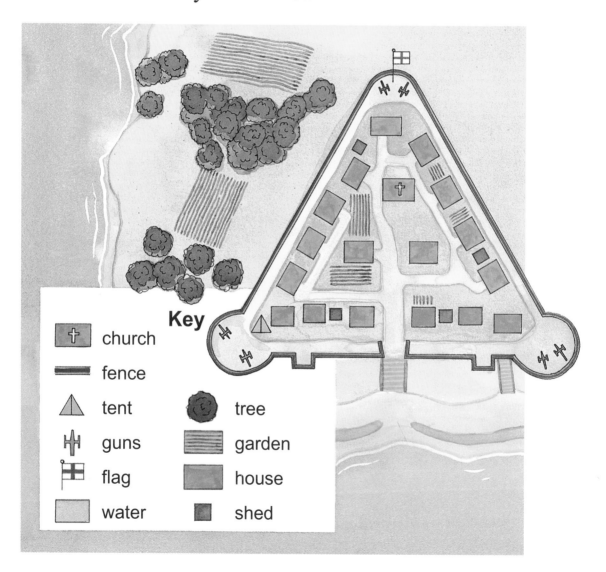

Key

| | | | |
|---|---|---|---|
| ✝ | church | | |
| ▬ | fence | | |
| ◮ | tent | ● | tree |
| ⚏ | guns | ▤ | garden |
| ⚑ | flag | ▦ | house |
| ▢ | water | ▪ | shed |

*Except the Lord keep the city, the watchman waketh but in vain.*

Psalm 127:1

## Plymouth Plantation

The Separatists chose to make their village like this.

Why do you think it is near the water?

Does this village look like Jamestown?

Can you find the fort?

A fort is like a lookout tower with guns.

People can go there to be safe.

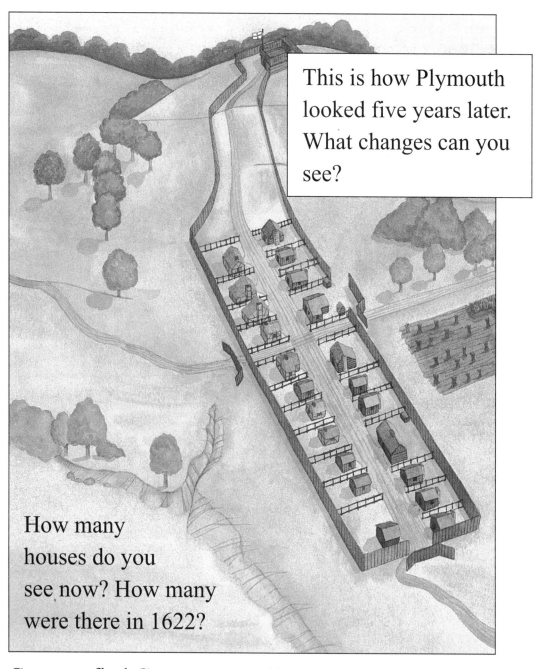

This is how Plymouth looked five years later. What changes can you see?

How many houses do you see now? How many were there in 1622?

Can you find Governor Bradford's house?
Are the corn fields like the ones where
Squanto lived?

84

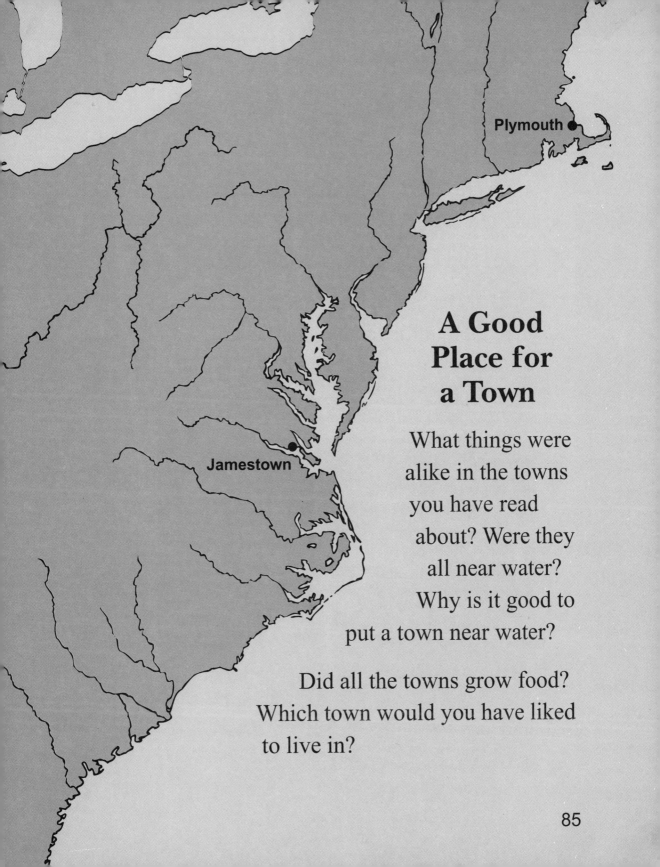

Plymouth

Jamestown

# A Good
# Place for
# a Town

What things were
alike in the towns
you have read
about? Were they
all near water?
Why is it good to
put a town near water?

Did all the towns grow food?
Which town would you have liked
to live in?

# To Plan a Village

1. Get your Notebook page, some scissors, some crayons, some glue, and a felt-tip marker.

2. Color and cut out the model houses, storehouse, and fort.

3. Glue the buildings onto the map. Why did you choose the spots you did? Color the whole map. Name the settlement.

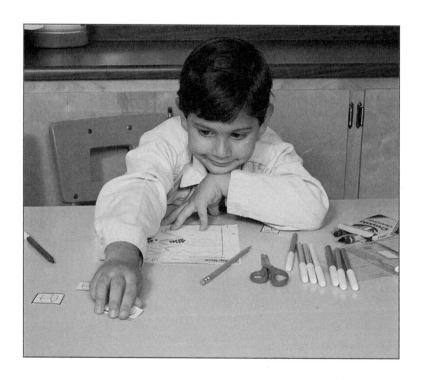

# 7

# Schools Then and Now

What kind of school do you go to?

What do you learn in school?

Why do you think it is important to go to school?

School has always been important in America.
Soon after the Pilgrims came,
they began schools.

*Seek ye out of the book of the Lord, and read.*
Isaiah 34:16

Some children went to *dame schools* or
*kitchen schools.*
Women taught these schools. Women were
called *dames* in those days.
These schools were held in the kitchens.

Sometimes children went to a neighbor's house
for school.
The parents took turns teaching
each other's children.

In Plymouth Plantation the law said all parents must teach their children to read.
Why do you think that was the law?

The Plymouth leaders wanted everyone to read the Bible for himself.
Why do you think reading the Bible was important to the people?

A law in Boston said that towns with
one hundred families should build a school.
These schools had one teacher for the children
of many families.
Can you find the school for many children on
the map?

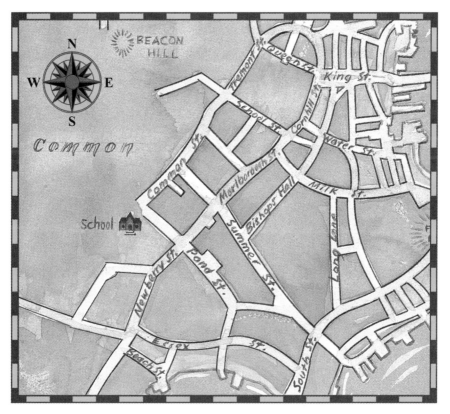

How do you think the towns paid the teachers?
Everyone in town had to give some money to
help pay the teacher.

Do you think the children in schools long ago had books and paper as you have?

Most schools had a special kind of book called a *hornbook.*

The hornbook looked like a wooden paddle.

It had a piece of paper on it.

What do you think was on the paper?

The hornbook had the Lord's Prayer on it.
It had the letters of the alphabet
on it.
Children sometimes wore
the book on a string
around their necks.
Then they could learn their
letters while they did chores.
They could
hold the book
in one hand
and feed the chickens
with the other.

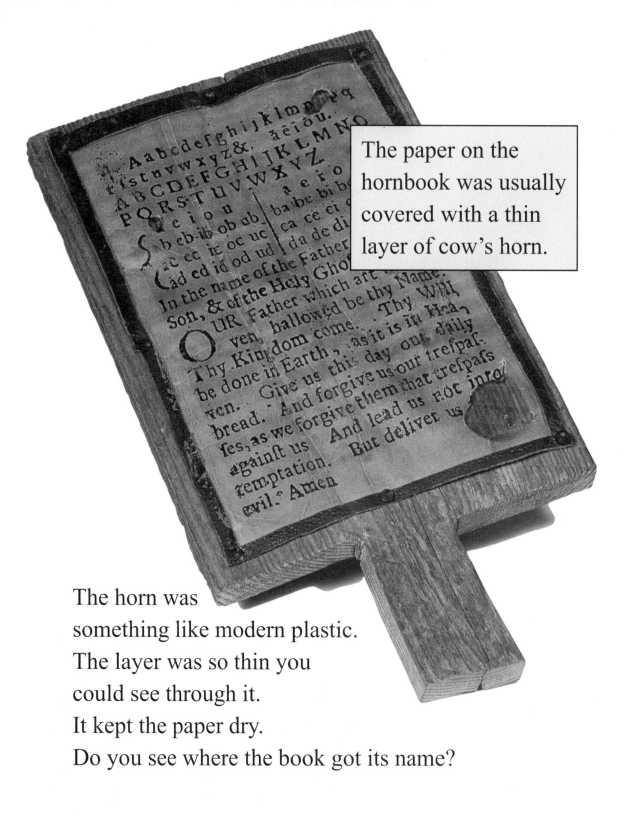

The paper on the hornbook was usually covered with a thin layer of cow's horn.

The horn was something like modern plastic. The layer was so thin you could see through it. It kept the paper dry. Do you see where the book got its name?

# To Make a Hornbook

1. Get a piece of cardboard, your Notebook pages, a piece of stiff plastic or plastic wrap, a pair of scissors, some string, a hole puncher, and some glue.

2. Cut out the hornbook pattern from the Notebook page. Cut the cardboard using the pattern.

3. Cut out the hornbook page from the Notebook page. Glue it onto the cardboard as your teacher shows you.

4. Punch a hole at the end of the handle. Put the string through the hole and tie the ends.

5. Glue the plastic over the hornbook page. Now hold out your "hornbook." Can you read the letters?

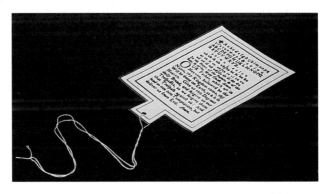

What kind of books do you have in your school?
Do you ever wear them around your neck?
Do you think you would like to learn
from a hornbook?

How else is your school different from the
schools in Plymouth and Boston?
Is anything the same?

You go to school to learn to read and write.
Why do you need to learn to read and write?

Who is your teacher?
Is your teacher like a kitchen school teacher or
a Boston teacher of many children?

Not all schools are the same today.
Some are like kitchen schools.
Some are like the schools built for
many children.

Some teachers of many children are paid
by churches.
Others are paid by the towns they live in.
The money paid by towns comes from *taxes*.

Taxes are what people pay to help their towns or
cities build schools and pay teachers.
Taxes also help pay for hospitals and
fire stations.

Taxes help pay for . . .

schools     hospitals     fire stations

▶ Do you remember how teachers were paid in
early America?

# Making Laws

When people live in the same place, they
need laws.
The laws help them live together
without fighting.
Most groups of people choose people to make
their laws.

The early Americans in Massachusetts had a
*General Court.*
The court was made up of several men who
were wise.
What law about schools did the
General Court make?

Today our laws are made
by people we vote for.
It is important to vote for
people who will make
good laws.

99

## To Vote About Rules

1. Get a small piece of paper and a pencil.

2. Make up some rules for your classroom. Your teacher will write them out on chart paper or on the chalkboard.

3. Vote for the rule you think is best for your classroom. Write the number of the rule on your paper.

# 8

# Trading
# with the Indians

The men who first sailed to the northern part
of the New World were not interested in
everything there.
They wanted to make maps of the coast.
They wanted to fish in the cool ocean water.
They wanted to settle along the calm rivers
and streams.

Soon the mapmakers and fishermen learned that
the Indians wanted things they had.
And the Indians learned that the white men
wanted things they had too.
What do you think the men did when they
learned these things?

# Trading Things

*And they brought their cattle unto Joseph: and Joseph gave them bread in exchange.*

Genesis 47:17

Long ago, people got most things they had
to have from the land.
Other things they got by *trading*.

*Trading* means giving one thing to get another.
Some people still trade things today.
Friends might trade toys.
And sometimes children trade food in the
lunchroom.
Have you ever traded
anything with someone?

The Indians came to the white men first.
They asked the white men for iron tools and
brightly colored cloth.
Did the white men just
give these things
to the Indians?

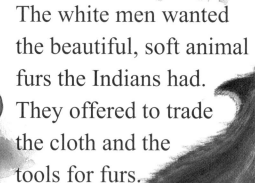

The white men wanted
the beautiful, soft animal
furs the Indians had.
They offered to trade
the cloth and the
tools for furs.

The Indians agreed to trade.
They knew where to get more soft furs.
But they did not know how to make the cloth or
iron tools.

Do you think the white men kept the warm furs?
The men sent most of the furs to lands across
the ocean.
The men traded the furs for food and other
things they had to have to live.
They traded the furs for things they wanted.
What do you think they used these things for?
They used them to trade with the Indians again.

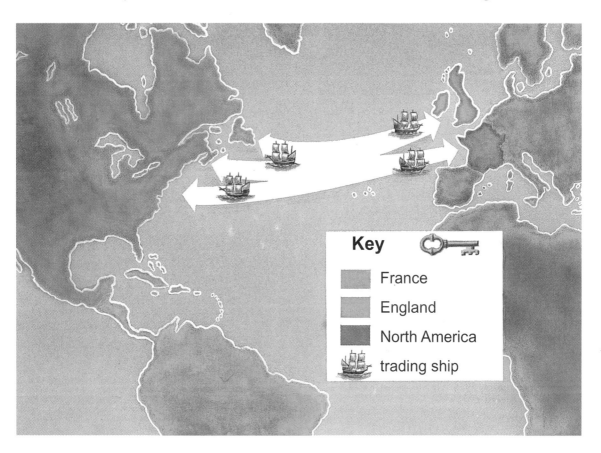

Key

France
England
North America
trading ship

# Making Things from Animal Skins

The Indians made many things from the animal furs.

They sewed furs together to make warm blankets and coats.

But most often Indian women scraped the fur from the skin.

They used these skins to make clothes and special shoes called *moccasins*.

Do you think the white men used the furs in the same way?

They did not make many blankets from fur.

They did not scrape the fur from the skins.

But they did make coats from the fur.

What other things do you think they made?

# Pierre Esprit Radisson

Pierre Radisson was only sixteen years old when he was captured and adopted by Iroquois. Pierre learned about the Indians while he lived with them.

He learned the Iroquois language.
He learned to hunt for food and to live in the wilderness.
He learned how the Iroquois made war and how they made peace.

When Pierre became a man, he traded with many groups of Indians.
He helped to set up trading companies in New France and New England.
And he helped to build a friendship between the Indians and the Frenchmen.

The first settlers traded for things too.
But they did not trade for furs with the Indians.
Mostly they traded with other settlers.
Someone who made lovely cloth could trade
with someone who made sturdy shoes.
Or someone who had extra wood might trade
with someone who had extra food.

The settlers knew that some things were
wanted by many people.
Many people wanted nails, bullets,
and a plant called tobacco.
Things that many people wanted
were worth more.
A settler who had one of
these special things
could trade it for
almost anything.

The settlers did trade with the Indians for
some things.
But sometimes the Indians did not want what
the settlers had.
And sometimes the settlers did not want what
the Indians had.
What do you think the settlers and Indians
did then?

The Indians had a kind of money with a very long name.
The settlers shortened the name to *wampum*. They learned to use wampum to get things they wanted.

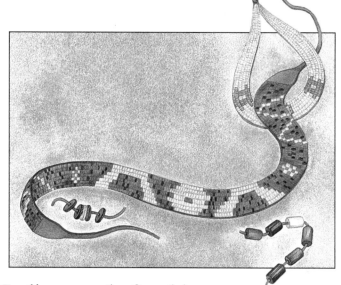

And they gladly let the Indians trade for things with more wampum.
What do you think the settlers did when they got more wampum from the Indians?

Do you know what the wampum was made from?
The Indians made it from polished seashells.
They cut the shells so that they were all the same size.
Then they put the wampum on strings like beads.
The wampum was purple and black and white.
Which wampum do you think was worth the most? Black was.

## To Make a Wampum Necklace

1. Gather some hollow macaroni pieces, food coloring, a bowl, water, and heavy string or yarn.

2. Fill the bowl with water. Add a few drops of food coloring.

3. Soak the macaroni pieces in the water. (Do not soak the pieces too long or the macaroni will become mushy.) Take the pieces from the water and lay them out to dry.

4. Make a wampum necklace or bracelet by threading the pieces of macaroni on the string. How is your wampum different from the Indians' wampum?

Today we do not use wampum,
jewelry, and guns for trading.
But we still trade to get things we want.
What do we use for our trading?
We trade coins and dollar bills for the things
we want.
Trading is much easier when everyone uses the
same thing.

# 9
# Adventurers

People in the Old World liked the goods that came from the New World.
They liked the gold, the new kinds of food, and the tobacco.

They especially liked the beautiful furs of beavers and foxes.
What do you think they used the furs for?
People wanted the furs to make clothes.

France and England sent men to explore more
of the New World.
These men went to find more furs
and other goods.
They went into the forests.
They went down big rivers.
They met many different Indian people.

Did these explorers travel before or after
Columbus made his trip?
Was Jamestown already built?

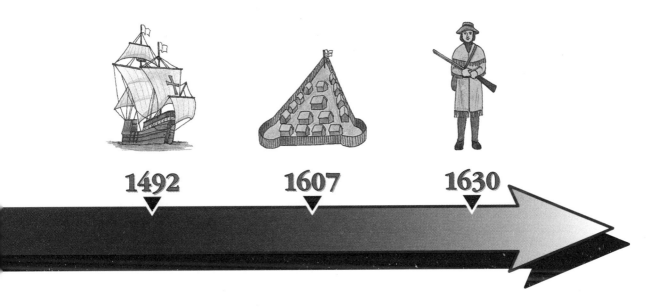

1492          1607          1630

The explorers came back to France and England.
They told about their adventures
in the New World.
They told of trees so big that five men could not
reach around them.
They told about snow so deep that it could
cover houses.
They said hunting was easy because birds and
animals were everywhere.

One French boy named Robert La Salle listened
to stories about the big forests and the strange
animals called buffaloes and moose.

He listened to tales
about a river so huge
that it looked like
an ocean.
The river was called
*Mississippi.*
The name came from
two Indian words
meaning "Big River."

La Salle had always wanted to go
on an adventure.
In school he had dreamed of sailing to America.
La Salle's brother was already in the New World.
He was a Catholic priest.

When La Salle grew up, he did not want to buy
and sell goods.
La Salle did not want to be a priest.
He did not want any gold.
He did not want to be a fur trader.
What do you think he wanted?

La Salle wanted to see parts of the New World
that no white man had ever seen.
He wanted to be the first to find where the
Mississippi River ended.

King Louis wanted everyone to know he was a
powerful king.
The king told La Salle to take men and ships
to the New World.
He told La Salle that any land he saw first would
belong to France.
He ordered La Salle to build forts
on the new lands.

# Louis the Fourteenth

Louis the Fourteenth was a king of France.
How many kings named Louis came before him?
He called himself the "sun king."
Sometimes he dressed
in gold clothes and
painted his face
gold.
He made life hard
for the Christians
in France.
Many of them
left.
Louis was sorry
to lose the best
workers in
France.

*When the righteous are in
authority, the people rejoice:
but when the wicked beareth
rule, the people mourn.*

Proverbs 29:2

119

## Playing Chess

Most people play chess on a game board similar to a checker board. King Louis the Fourteenth played on a much bigger one. His chess board was a whole lawn.
His chess pieces were
real people and horses.

La Salle and his men traveled into
the New World.
They canoed down streams and rivers.
The winter snows came, and the food ran out.
Some men wanted to go back.
La Salle refused to give up.
What do you think he did?

He asked the Indians for help.
The Illinois Indians fed La Salle and his men.
La Salle gave the Illinois Indians axes and
knives in return.
He learned to speak different Indian
languages well.
He always kept his promises with everyone.

The Indians trusted La Salle.

They told him how to find the Mississippi River.

La Salle and a few men went down the big river in canoes.

At last they came to the end.

La Salle found what he was looking for.

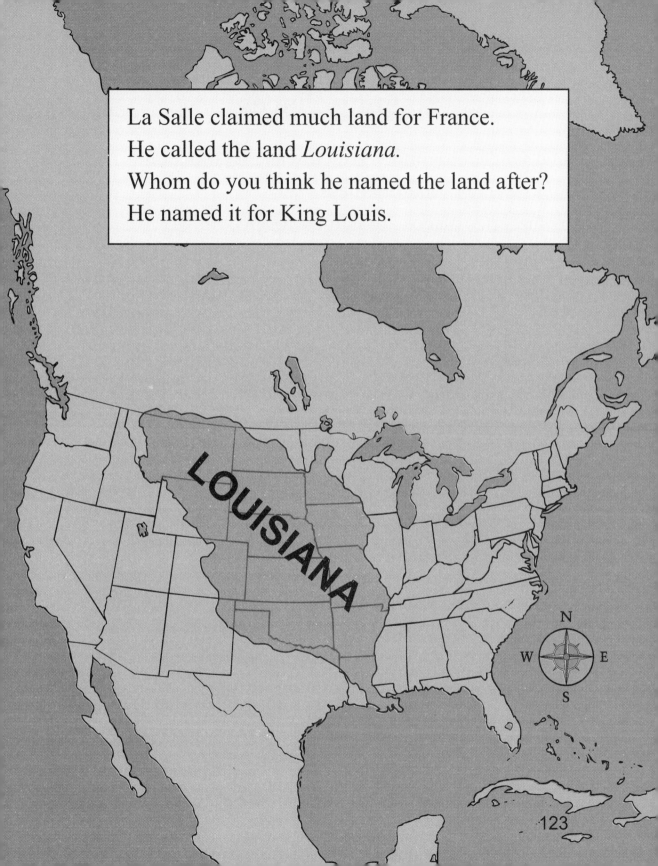

La Salle claimed much land for France.
He called the land *Louisiana.*
Whom do you think he named the land after?
He named it for King Louis.

LOUISIANA

N
W E
S

123

# Naming Places

Did you ever wonder how towns and mountains
and rivers got their names?
Sometimes places are named for people.
Can you think of a place named for a person?
Sometimes places are named for how they look.
How do you think the river Big Muddy looks?
How do you think the city on this map
got its name?

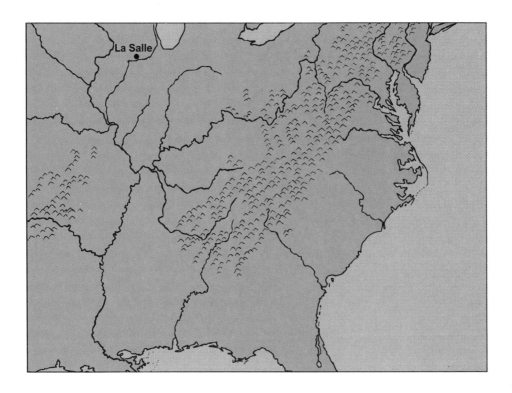

## To Name Places

1. Get your Notebook and a pencil.

2. Make up names for the places your teacher tells you about.

3. Tell the names of your places to a friend. Can he guess why you chose the names you did?

What do you think makes
cities different from each other?
People bring different ways
to places.
They bring different ways
of cooking and speaking.
How do you think the
cities La Salle started
were different from
Jamestown?

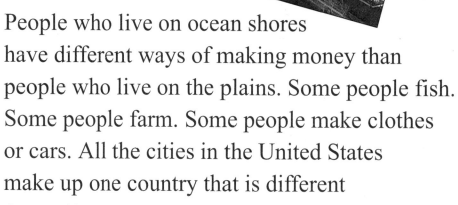

People who live on ocean shores
have different ways of making money than
people who live on the plains. Some people fish.
Some people farm. Some people make clothes
or cars. All the cities in the United States
make up one country that is different
from all other countries
in the world. What
makes your
town or city
special?

# 10

# The One True God

How do you believe people can get to heaven?
Not everyone believes the same way.
There are many beliefs about God and about
how to get to heaven.
There are even many different
beliefs about what heaven is.
The beliefs about God and
heaven are called *religions*.

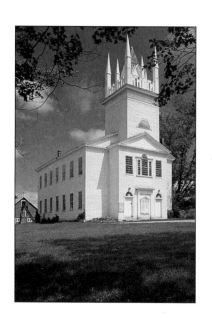

*I am the Lord, and there is none else, there is no God
beside me.*

Isaiah 45:5

The Bible says that God is the only God.
The Bible says that believing on Jesus is the only way to heaven.
Some religions say that doing good will help get you to heaven.
Is that true?

# Other Gods in the New World

Many Indian peoples lived in the New World.
None of them knew about the God of the Bible.

Some tribes worshiped the stars and the moon.
Some worshiped animals or carved pieces
of wood.

People coming to the New World brought other
ideas about gods.
People called *Vikings* had gods of thunder
and wind.
People from Africa and Mexico had stone gods.

# Religions in the New World

Many of the white men who traded with the
Indians had their own beliefs about God.
Some traders were Roman Catholics.
They said that Jesus Christ is God and that
He died for our sins.
They believed that you get to heaven
by believing in Christ and by
belonging to the
Catholic Church.

> *Not by works of righteousness
> which we have done, but according
> to his mercy he saved us.*
>
> Titus 3:5

Roman Catholics have a leader called the *pope*.
Many believe that some things the pope says are
as true as what the Bible says.
Is any man as wise as God?

Most Indians kept their old religions.
They did not take the white man's gods.
Others took part of the Roman Catholic religion.

Today many people in America think that to get
to heaven they just have to live a good life.
These people need to hear the truth.
How will they hear?

# The Puritans and the Separatists

Many of the countries that sent people to the
New World were Roman Catholic.
Most of the French people were Roman Catholic.
Most of the Spanish people were

Roman Catholic.
Those countries
followed the pope.
England had some
Roman Catholics.
But England did not
follow the pope.
England had its
own church.

Some people in England believed the Bible.
These people wanted to make the English
churches completely different from the Roman
Catholic churches. These people said they
wanted to make the churches in England pure.
They were called the *Puritans*.

# To Sing a Puritan Hymn

1. Take out your Notebook.

2. Listen to the tune your teacher sings or plays for you.

3. Sing the words of the Puritan hymn with the tune. Where do you think the words of the hymn come from?

The Puritans could not make the churches pure. So some Puritans decided to leave England and go to a new place. Do you remember who these people were?

Why do you think they were called Separatists?

They "separated" from the church they did not think was pure.

Some of them came to the New World.

Look at the line on this page.

Did the Separatists come to the New World before or after Columbus?

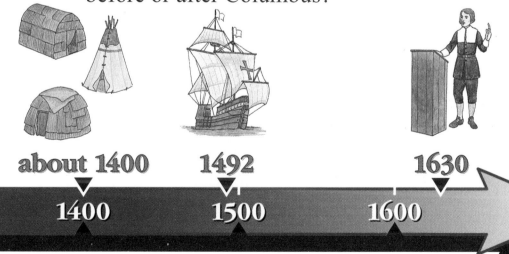

about 1400        1492                          1630

1400              1500              1600

Some people call the Separatists *Pilgrims*.
Pilgrims are people who travel to other places.
There were other travelers on the *Mayflower*
besides Separatists.
Some Pilgrims were people who sold things;
some were people who were running away from
hard masters.

The Separatists believed that faith in Christ was the only way to heaven.

The Separatists built their own churches.

They sang hymns.

They heard sermons about how God wants people to live.

They read the Bible and obeyed God.

The church leaders helped make rules for the towns.

Today our coins say "In God we trust."

Why do you think our country began with a belief in God?

The Separatists worked hard.
Their towns grew. They made money.
They knew that every blessing came
from God.

Later settlers also
worked hard.
America became
a rich, strong
country.

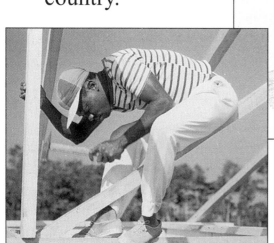

How do you think the early settlers helped
make America what it is?
Do you think that Americans still believe
that hard work will bring good results?

# 11

# People Have Needs and Wants

Long ago, people came to America.
Traders came. Pilgrims came.
Explorers came.
Did they come empty-handed?
No, they brought with them many things.
What kinds of things did they bring?
They brought things they needed to live
in a new land.

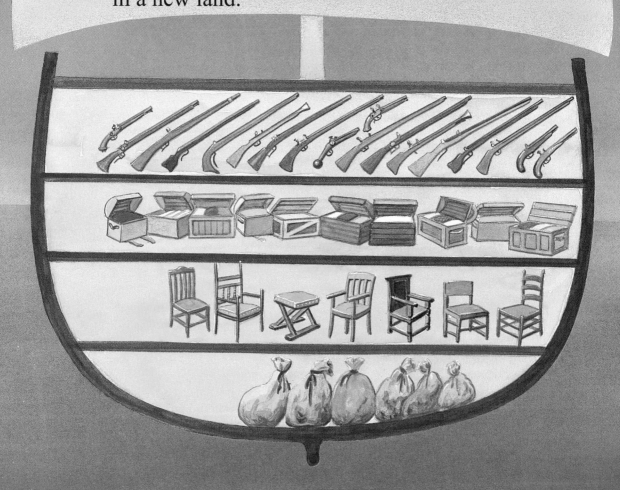

# Things People Need

People everywhere have needs.
*Needs* are the things people must have to live.
What things do you need to live?
You need food.
You need a place to live.
You need clothes to wear.
And you need care and love
from other people.

*For your heavenly Father knoweth that ye
have need of all these things.*

Matthew 6:32

# You Need Food

People everywhere need food.
Food helps us to grow healthy and strong.
We need many kinds of food to help us grow.
What kind of food do you like to eat?

Some people grow their own food. Some people buy most of their food in a store.

Do you know where the food in the store comes from?

Someone grew the food on a farm.

Perhaps someone else prepared it in a factory.

# You Need Shelter

People everywhere need
a place to live.
We call this place to live
a *shelter.*

What does your home
look like?
Your home is a shelter.
It protects you from cold weather.
It protects you from rain.
It keeps you dry and warm.
What things do you do in your home?

## You Need Clothes

People everywhere need clothes.
Clothes help to protect us from heat, cold, and rain.
These things make up *weather.*

Some people must have clothes for warm weather and cold weather.
These people live where the weather changes with the seasons.
The seasons are winter, spring, summer, and fall.
Does the weather change with the seasons where you live?
Do you have clothes for more than one season?

Where do people get the clothes they need?
Some people buy their clothes in a store.
These clothes have been made by other people.
Some people make their own clothes.
Do you have any clothes that were made especially for you?

## You Need Love and Care

People everywhere need love and care.

They need to love and care for others too.

Who loves and cares for you?

Your family and friends do.

God loves and cares for you too.

How do your family and friends show that they
love you?

They can do something special for you.

They can do something special with you.

People have many ways to show others that
they care. How can you show people that you
love and care for them?

# Things People Want

People everywhere have wants.

*Wants* are things that we would like to have.

But we do not need them.

Do you get everything you want?

You must often decide which things you want the most.

Do you want the same things that your friend wants? Probably not.

All people have the same needs, but they do not always have the same wants.

# Getting Needs and Wants

Long ago, people traded things they made or
grew to get other things.
In this way, they got the things they needed
and wanted.

Today we use money to pay for the things we
need and want.
But we cannot grow money or make money.
How can we get money?
People get money by working.

## Saving Money

Have you ever needed or wanted something that
cost a lot of money?
How might you get enough money to buy it?
You could save small amounts of money.
Soon you would have enough to buy what

you wanted.

Adults save money
in buildings that look
like this.

Children save money in places like that too.

More often children
save money in places
like this.

What do we call
these kinds of places? We call them *banks*.
Banks are a safe place to save money.

152

Many people make a plan for spending
their money.
This plan is called a *budget*.
When people follow their budget, they can buy
the things they need.
They may even have money left to buy some of
the things they want.

*Delight thyself also in the Lord; and he shall give thee
the desires of thine heart.*

Psalm 37:4

# To Make a Budget

1. Get a pencil and your Notebook.

2. Pretend that you earn a 50-cent allowance each week. Make a list of the things you need. Make another list of the things you want. Decide how you should spend your money each week.

3. Write the things you need and want. Record the amount of money you can spend on each thing during the week. Remember to give some of your money to God. Make sure that you do not spend more than 50 cents during the week.

# 12

## Families Together

Is there anyone on Earth just like you?

No, you are special.

What things about you are special?

No one looks just like you.

No one thinks just like you.

No one acts just like you.

God made you different from everyone else.

You are an *individual*.

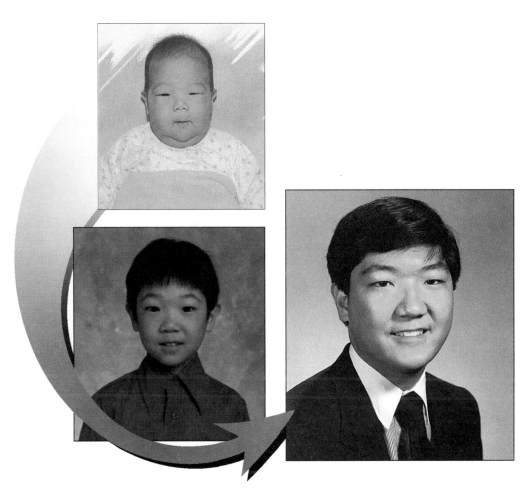

Have you always looked the way you do today?
When you were a baby, you were much smaller.
You began to change as you got older.
You will keep growing until you are much older.

As you grew, you learned to do many things.
What things have you learned?
What things would you still like to learn?

# To Make a Height Chart

1. Get a yardstick, a roll of paper, tape or Plasti-Tak, and a pencil.

2. Fasten the paper to the wall using tape or Plasti-Tak. Stand with your back to the paper. Make sure that your heels are against the wall.

3. With the help of your teacher or a friend, mark your height on the paper. Place the yardstick on top of your head and let it touch the wall to show where to draw a line. Write your name and the date next to the mark.

4. Use the yardstick to measure from the floor to the line. How tall are you?

# A Family Is Special

A *family* is a special group of people.
A family is special because each person in the family is an individual.
No other family is just like your family.
God gave you your family.

Some families are very large.
Some families are very small.
How many people are in your family?

God created the first man and woman.
Adam and Eve became the first family.
Do you remember the names of their children?

People have always lived together as families.
God planned for families to live and
work together.

# A Family Changes

A family changes as time goes by.
*Change* means that things are different from
what they were before.
In what ways has your family changed?

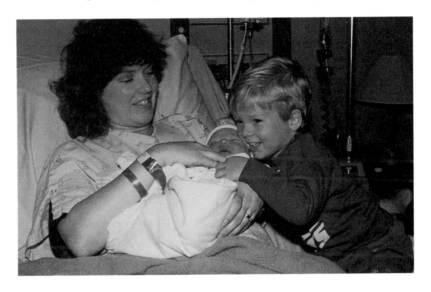

Families change in many ways.
Adding a new brother or sister can change
a family.
Moving to a new home brings changes too.
All families change in one way.
They change as the people in the family
grow older.

# A Family Has Rules

All families have rules.

Rules can help you know what you should do.

Rules can help you know what you must not do.

Do you know why we need rules?

Rules help us get along with others.

And rules help to protect us from harm.

What rules does your family have?

Who makes your rules?

*Children, obey your parents in the Lord: for this is right.*

Ephesians 6:1

Sometimes families need to make new rules
or change old ones.
How does your family decide on changes
like these?

A family might talk about the reasons for
changing a rule.
They might list the reasons for the change.
Each family member may even *vote* for or
against the new rule.
Have you ever helped to make a rule?

## Voting

In some countries, people choose the rules they think are right.
They choose the leaders that they think will make the best rules.
People make their choices known by *voting*.

A person can vote by writing his choice on a piece of paper.
A person can vote by raising his hand.

When a choice must be made by many people, a special day is set aside for voting.
People mark their votes on special pieces of paper or special machines.

# A Family Works and Plays Together

Families do things together.

The people in a family do things for each other.

They show their love for each other.

Families work together.

Working together makes the work easier.

Working together gets the job done faster.

Any work you do can be called a *job.*

What jobs do you do for your family?

Families play together.
What things does your family do together
for fun?

Christian families
do something
else together.
They worship
God together.
How do we
worship God?

# A Family Has a History

*History* is the story of people and the things they have done. We often think of history as the story of famous people.

Famous people have a history.
But people who are not famous have a history too.

All families have a history.
Your family's history is the story of the people in your family who came before you.
Those family members are called *ancestors*.
Your parents and grandparents are your ancestors.
What do you know about the things they have done?

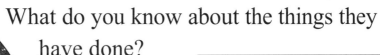

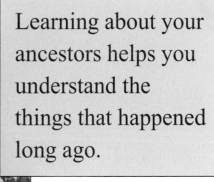

Learning about your ancestors helps you understand the things that happened long ago.

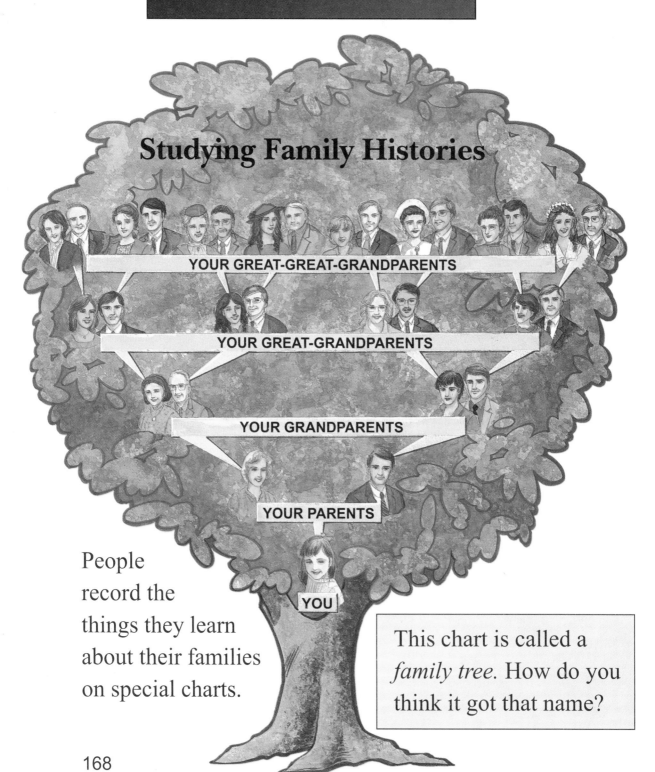

## Studying Family Histories

YOUR GREAT-GREAT-GRANDPARENTS

YOUR GREAT-GRANDPARENTS

YOUR GRANDPARENTS

YOUR PARENTS

YOU

People record the things they learn about their families on special charts.

This chart is called a *family tree*. How do you think it got that name?

# To Record Your Personal History

1. Take out a pencil, some crayons, several sheets of paper, and some tape or yarn.

2. Draw pictures showing things you have done and things that have happened to you.

3. Put your drawings into the order that they happened. Hang your drawings in this order, or make your own personal history book.

Your family's history is your story too.
You have done things.
You may not have discovered a new land or led
a group of people, but you have a history.
What do you know about your history?

Each day you make a little more of your history.
The things you do become part of your history.
They become part of your family's history.
What kind of story will people tell about you?

*Even a child is known by his doings, whether his work*
*be pure, and whether it be right.*

Proverbs 20:11

# Resource
# Treasury

# Plymouth Rock

This spot may be where the *Mayflower* landed.

You can visit a new Plymouth Plantation.

# *Mayflower*

This is an exact copy of the ship the Separatists sailed on.

Would you like to sail to England on this *Mayflower?*

How does it look compared to a modern ship?

# The Bible of Plymouth Plantation

This is a Geneva Bible.

This is the kind of Bible that the Separatists brought to New England.

It was the first Bible in English to have the verses numbered.

The print in this Bible was easy to read.

Many English families owned a Bible like this.

# Columbus Day

The first Columbus Day was October 12, 1492. One of Columbus's men saw land on that day. Columbus and his men had been sailing for more than thirty days.

Would you like to take a trip on a ship like Columbus's?

# Foods the Indians Gave Us

Indians taught the white men what foods to plant.
They gave them seeds for all these foods.

# Totem Poles

Indians did not worship the true God.
Sometimes they worshiped animals.
They carved the animals in tall poles.

# A Family Tree

Some people keep information on everyone who has ever been in their families. They use *family trees* to record information.

Here is a family tree for one person in New England. Do you think it looks like a tree?

# The United States Today

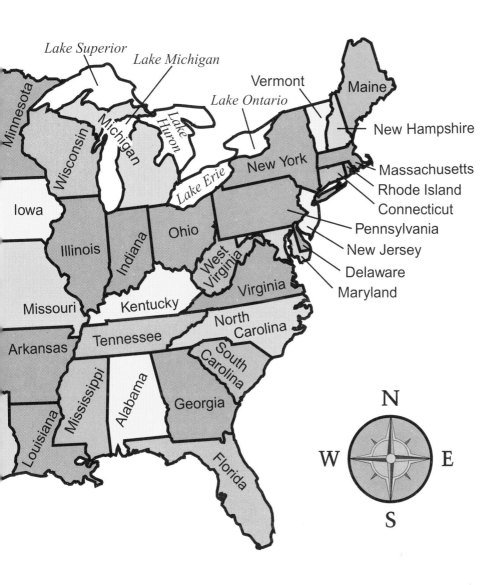

Lake Superior
Lake Michigan
Lake Ontario
Vermont
Maine
Lake Huron
New Hampshire
Lake Erie
Massachusetts
Rhode Island
Connecticut
Pennsylvania
New Jersey
Delaware
Maryland

Minnesota
Wisconsin
Michigan
New York
Iowa
Illinois
Indiana
Ohio
West Virginia
Virginia
Missouri
Kentucky
North Carolina
Arkansas
Tennessee
South Carolina
Mississippi
Alabama
Georgia
Louisiana
Florida

N
W        E
S

Hawaii

# Indian Nations of Long Ago

When Columbus came, many Indians lived in what is now the United States.

How many different Indian groups does the map show?

**Key**

1. Aleut
2. Eskimo
3. Hare
4. Dogrib
5. Tlingit
6. Nootka
7. Chippewa
8. Cree
9. Lillouet
10. Blackfoot
11. Algonquin

12. Iroquois
13. Nez Perce
14. Sioux
15. Fox
16. Potawatomi
17. Tolowa
18. Shoshone
19. Crow
20. Pawnee
21. Shawnee
22. Pedee

23. Yuma
24. Navajo
25. Hopi
26. Comanche
27. Kiowa
28. Caddo
29. Natchez
30. Choctaw
31. Seminole
32. Carib
33. Arawak

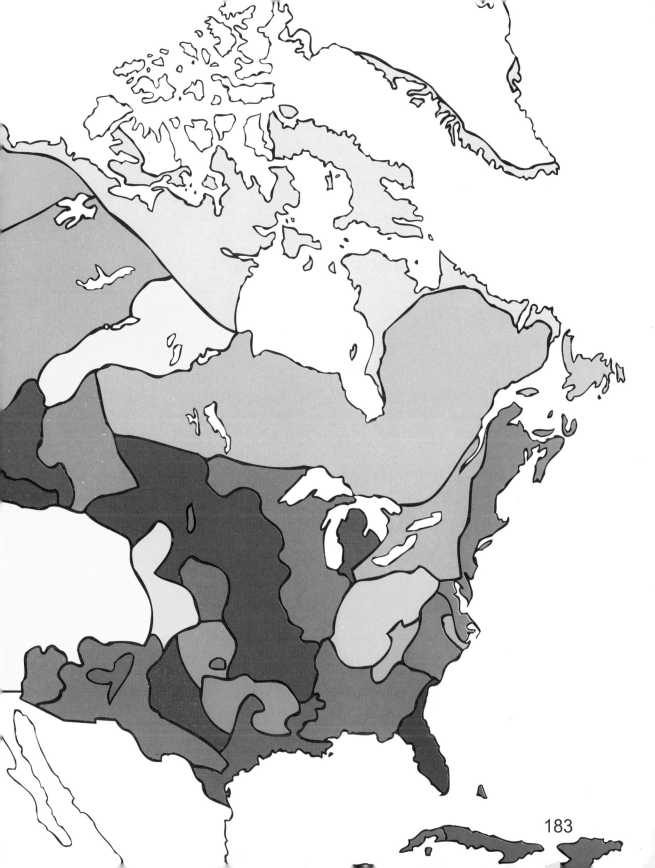

# Geogloss

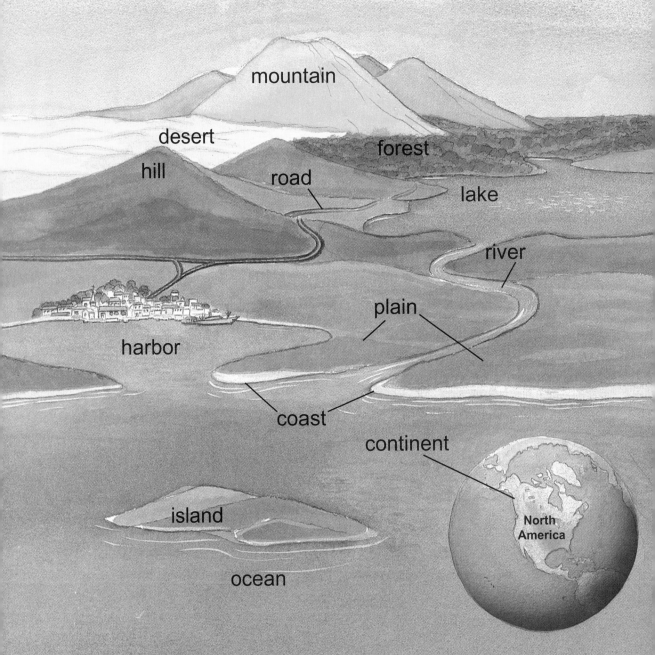

mountain

desert

hill

forest

road

lake

river

harbor

plain

coast

continent

North America

island

ocean

# Picture Glossary

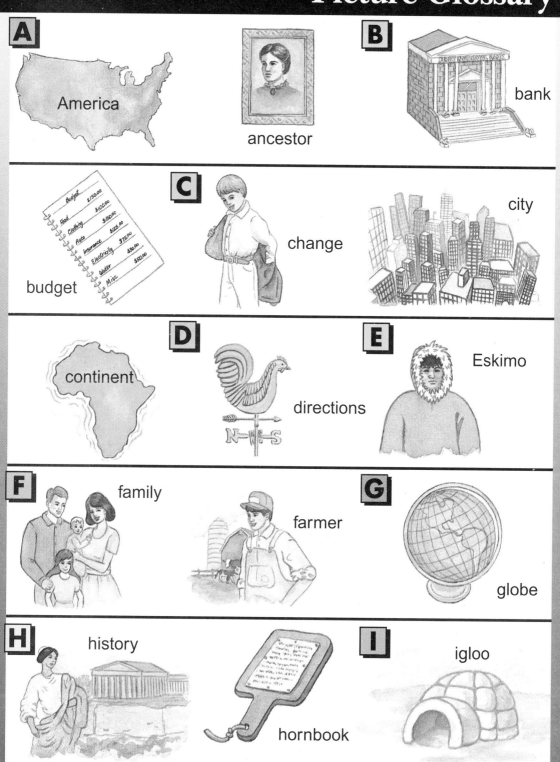

**A**

America

ancestor

**B**

bank

budget

**C**

change

city

**D**

continent

directions

**E**

Eskimo

**F**

family

farmer

**G**

globe

**H**

history

hornbook

**I**

igloo

# Picture Glossary

India

Indian

J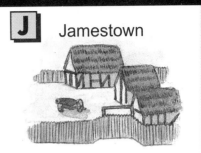
Jamestown

job

M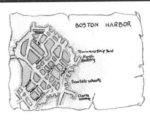
map

*Mayflower*

Mississippi River

moccasin

N
needs

New World

North America

O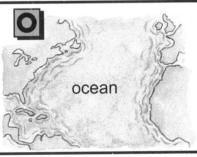
ocean

P
pilgrim

Plymouth Plantation

pope

# Picture Glossary

 Puritan

**R** religion

rule

**S** Separatist

settlement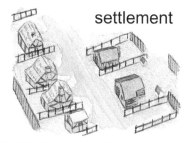

shelter

**T** tax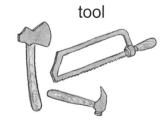

Thanksgiving

tipi

tool

trade

**V** Virginia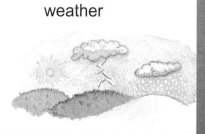

vote

**W** wampum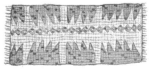

weather

# Photograph Credits

The following agencies and individuals have furnished materials to meet the photographic needs of this textbook. We wish to express our gratitude to them for their important contribution.

Stewart Aitchison
Suzanne R. Altizer
The Boston Athanaeum
Wes Breedlove
George R. Buckley
George R. Collins
Terry Davenport
Department of the Army
Eastman Chemicals Division
Sharon Higgs

International Apple Institute
Italian Tourist Agency
Brian Johnson
Library of Congress
Massachusetts Office of Travel
   and Tourism
National Gallery of Art
National Park Service
John M. Nolan
Edward S. Park

Debbie Parker
Kathy Pflug
Becky J. Smith
Kim Stegall
United States Department of
   Agriculture (USDA)
Unusual Films
Kay Washer
Dawn L. Watkins
World Bank

**Cover/Title page**
Dawn L. Watkins (all)

**Chapter 1**
Terry Davenport 1; George R. Collins 2 (top); Dawn L. Watkins 2 (bottom); Unusual Films 3, 7, 11, 14

**Chapter 2**
Brian Johnson 15; Unusual Films 19 (both); Kim Stegall 24

**Chapter 3**
Terry Davenport 29; Courtesy of Debbie Parker (arrowheads), Sharon Higgs (peace pipe), and Wes Breedlove 33; George R. Collins 35, 39; Brian Johnson 37; Unusual Films 43, 44

**Chapter 4**
George R. Collins 45; USDA 55; Unusual Films 57 (all)

**Chapter 5**
Unusual Films 59, 72; George R. Collins 65; Edward S. Park 71

**Chapter 6**
George R. Collins 73, 74, 79 (inset); Library of Congress 74 (inset); Eastman Chemicals Division 75; George R. Buckley 76; National Park Service 77; Brian Johnson 79; Stewart Aitchison 80; Unusual Films 86

**Chapter 7**
The Boston Athanaeum 87; Unusual Films 88, 92, 94, 95, 96, 97 (all), 98 (left, middle), 100; Suzanne R. Altizer 98 (right), 99

**Chapter 8**
Dawn L. Watkins 101; George R. Collins 102; Unusual Films 103, 111, 112

**Chapter 9**
George R. Collins 113, 126 (middle left, bottom left, bottom right); Department of the Army 118; Unusual Films 125; Suzanne R. Altizer 126 (top)

**Chapter 10**
Unusual Films 127, 129, 134 (both), 137; George R. Buckley 128 (top, bottom); World Bank 128 (middle), 138; George R. Collins 128 (left), 132; Italian Tourist Agency 133

**Chapter 11**
Unusual Films 139, 142 (bottom inset), 144 (top inset), 145 (bottom inset), 148-49, 149 (top inset), 151, 152 (bottom), 154; Kay Washer 141 (top); Becky J. Smith 141 (bottom left); George R. Collins 141 (bottom right), 144-45, 146-47; USDA 142-43; Suzanne R. Altizer 142 (top inset), 143 (top inset), 148 (bottom inset); International Apple Institute 143 (right inset); Terry Davenport 144 (left inset), 146 (top inset), 148-49 (right inset); Kim Stegall 144 (bottom), 149 (bottom inset); Kathy Pflug 145 (top inset); Dawn L. Watkins 146 (bottom), 148 (top inset), 153; Edward S. Park 152 (top)

**Chapter 12**
Unusual Films 155, 156, 158, 159, 160, 162, 163, 164, 165 (right), 166 (both), 169, 170; Edward S. Park 157 (all); Kim Stegall 161; Terry Davenport 165 (left); National Gallery of Art 167 (top); Brian Johnson 167 (bottom left, bottom right)

**Resource Treasury**
Massachusetts Office of Travel and Tourism 171, 172 (both), 173 (top); John M. Nolan 173 (bottom); Unusual Films 174 (both)